Confessions of an

OVERSPENDER

Recognizing the Symptoms; Treating the Disorder;
Beginning a New Life

Ben Carlsen

Confessions of an

OVERSPENDER

Recognizing the Symptoms
Treating the Disorder
Beginning a New Life

Dr. Ben A. Carlsen, MBA

PALM
SPRINGS
PUBLISHING

PSP

New York, Miami, Los Angeles

Ben Carlsen

Confessions of an Overspender
by Ben Carlsen

Copyright © 2012
ISBN no: 978-1-62407-191-1
Library of Congress no: 2012915377

Published by **Palm Springs Publishing**
New York, Miami, Los Angeles
Printed in U.S.A.

Cover Design by Greg Borowski
Borowski Design
www.borowskidesign.com

PREFACE

Alright, I confess. I'm an overspender! So, I won't be lecturing you in this book or pointing fingers or shame or blame. Whew, that's out of the way.

I suspect that you purchased this book because you're an overspender too. Or perhaps you have a family member, co-worker, or friend you would like to understand or help. Possibly you have broader concerns about a society that is so materialistic and obsessed with consumerism. Whatever your motivation, I'm sure you'll find value in these pages.

I also feel an obligation to provide you with value so that I won't feel I'm contributing to your problem and so you won't feel you've – once again – overpaid, overspent, or made an unwise purchase. In this book you will be exposed to symptoms of overspending – financial, behavioral, psychological and medical. You will read some examples, learn some reasons for the problem, be asked to objectively evaluate yourself, and take action to modify your behavior.

Overspending is such a common problem that we can all relate. We've all made purchases that we shouldn't have, we've all spent more money than we should have and we've all regretted buying something.

Our overspending is generally a secret vice or habit. People are more guarded and dishonest about money than any aspect of their life. But in order to change we must be objective and we must shine the light of honesty on our problem. Confession is an acknowledgment and a powerful step toward recovery.

"Confession is good for the soul" as the saying goes. It may also be good for the pocketbook. As a friend of mine said: If you confess, you'll spend less!" Try it sometime.

ACKNOWLEDGMENTS

Special thanks to all who helped and/or stood by me in creating this book, and in particular:

Elsie Delva-Smith, Roberto Montanez, Greg Borowski, Krzysztof Bryniuk, Fausto Manzo, and Hendrick Ferguson. Also my brother Gary and my sister Arla who know me very well.

Ben Carlsen

TABLE of CONTENTS

INTRODUCTION

In this book you may recognize characteristics of your spouse, your children, your friends or most importantly, yourself. Yes, in America we generally share a common disorder-- we overspend! We learn to overspend at an early age. We watch our family and friends buy things they may not need, but desperately want. (Or even buy things they don't want or need!) We see them toil away at jobs to make a living, but they seldom make much progress because they overuse credit, overspend and under-save.

Our government sets a fine example. They spend trillions, waste billions, and although they make budgets they almost never live within them. As a result they borrow hundreds of billions to feed their spending addiction and to buy our votes, support and goodwill. (Doesn't seem to work too well.) This pattern of irresponsibility is not unique to the United States, but as we all know, may be worse in some European nations and certainly much of the developing world.

Perhaps you are unaccustomed to thinking your financial problems are indicative of a disease. That might require some thought. The fact is that disease is just that "dis-ease" a condition of not being at ease, or unhealthy.

If you're uneasy, or outright befuddled about your financial situation it can make you sick! Or at least not in an optimally healthy position.

In fact, many medical practitioners believe that overspending has its root in other compulsive or addictive behavior. And there are, indeed, many similarities. For example overspending can produce a "high" followed by a "crash" in mood. The euphoria created by buying something may soon be replaced by feelings of despair and guilt. Yes, overspending is certainly a problem, whether it's a bad habit, a compulsion, an addiction, or a disease.

Chapter One

SYMPTOMS

Ben Carlsen

SYMPTOMS of OVERSPENDING

As with every disease or disorder there are symptoms which can aid in diagnosis. In this chapter we will explore some of the most common ones associated with overspending. These days it's common to label every problem as a "disease" and it takes away responsibility for behavior. After all, how can I be responsible if I am suffering from a disease? Others will have to help me recover. For example, experts in the field of my pathology.

In this chapter we will begin by exploring some symptoms related to overspending. Whether these are causal, consequential, or merely associated is another matter.

The discussion is divided into two components. First the financial and behavioral elements and next the most prevalent associated medical symptoms.

THE FINANCIAL and BEHAVIORAL SYMPTOMS of OVERSPENDING

--You run out of money before the month ends

--You don't have a household or personal budget

--You have little savings or investments

--You carry credit card balances month-to-month

--You have high interest rate or sub-prime credit cards

--You carry more than three credit cards

--You don't have a "cash reserve" for emergencies

--You live in fear of an unexpected expense

--You're behind in your taxes

--You aren't able to save at least 10% of your income

--You don't contribute enough to your 401k to receive your employer's "match"

--You have lots of stuff you seldom or never use

--You pay late charges or overdraft fees

--Your utility bills are sky high

--Your car isn't paid for

--You drive an over-size gas-guzzling vehicle

--You can't afford to make necessary home repairs

--You have lots of gadgets and the latest products

--You have a mortgage that's bigger than you can afford

--You use your home equity as a "piggy bank" by refinancing and borrowing.

--You're a sucker for advertising and marketing

--You're a status seeker

--You're afraid to quit a job that you hate because you can't afford to

--You constantly worry about bills and creditors

--You borrow from friends, payday lenders, pawn shops, or others

--You're in arrears, default, penalty, foreclosure, litigation, on your debt(s)

--You skip buying necessities like medicine or insurance because of the cost

--Your closet looks like a branch of *Macy's*

--Your home looks like a Thrift Shop

--You have an unnecessarily large (or expensive) home or apartment

--You eat out frequently, and/or you patronize expensive restaurants

--You buy pricey items, and don't shop for bargains

--You're overly brand or label conscious

--You believe "you get what you pay for"

--Shopping is your "hobby"

--You have trouble leaving a store without buying something

--You feel guilty or remorseful about several or many of your purchases

--You're a shopaholic, an alcoholic or drug addict

--You can't pass up a sale or "bargain"

--You try to "buy" friends, companions or lovers

--You visit prostitutes or subscribe to porn sites

--Your *FICO score* is below 750

--You can't afford to send your kids to college

--You can't afford to take a vacation

--You can't retire

It's incredible, but this is only a partial list. It would be impossible to list all of the reasons, emotional, psychological, behavioral and physical, symptomatic of overspending and problematic personal finances. Of course just because you have one or two of these issues doesn't mean you are an addictive overspender. But if you see several items that apply to you it's probably time to take notice, acknowledge that you may have a problem, and resolve to take corrective action. We'll discuss all of this later in the book.

THE MEDICAL SYMPTOMS OF OVERSPENDING ADDICTION

I'm not a medical doctor. My doctorate is academic. However, my research revealed several medical symptoms associated with overspending. We can argue whether these medical conditions are causal or not. I suspect not. But the manifestation of disease or disorders can be physical, behavioral and/or psychological.

For example, let's say you're overweight. And you believe it's due to lack of exercise. And why don't you exercise? Because you're depressed. And why are you depressed? Because you don't exercise. You see it becomes circular, because problems and symptoms are interrelated. And symptoms frequently don't accurately point to the root cause. Problems and conditions affect people in different ways.

With overspending; do you do it because you have low self-esteem, because you're depressed, or anxious, or tired, or mentally confused, or obsessive-compulsive, or lack discipline and self-control, because you're easily manipulated, because you're optimistic or pessimistic, or you like the feeling it gives you, or because you're conforming to a cultural norm?

Most authorities agree the primary medical symptoms of overspenders include:

-Depression

-Anxiety

-Fatigue

-Insomnia

A website *"Patients like me"* has an Overspending Report which categorizes the compulsive spending malady by severity of symptoms.

Their report indicates that 25% are classified as Severe; 24% Moderate; 22% Mild; and 35% None. They indicate "Compulsive Spenders show many of the same symptoms as people suffering from more common addictions."

So we see that there are plenty of warnings, physical, mental and behavioral. Our overspending is not an innocent indulgence when it becomes habitual. And it does not occur in isolation. You probably never thought of your overspending as evidence of addiction or disease. And you probably didn't realize how intertwined our behaviors, physical and mental health are with our finances.

Your psychological and physical well-being can be influenced by your finances and vice-versa. If you're obsessive-compulsive or depressed, can't sleep, anxious or just "worn out" it can be indicative of, or resulting from your financial condition. And conversely, your finances are adversely impacted by these conditions. Next we'll delve further into the psychology of this affliction.

Ben Carlsen

Chapter Two

DIAGNOSIS

Ben Carlsen

DIAGNOSING THE PROBLEM

In addition to the behaviors and medical symptoms described in Chapter One there are excuses and rationalizations commonly used by those afflicted with the overspending malady. These psychological tricks can preserve our ego and self-image but prevent us from dealing with reality. We will take a look at some of the more common approaches.

EXCUSES

Are you an overspender? If you find yourself with some or many of the aforementioned symptoms you may very well be. Of course self-diagnosis is always dangerous. And I wouldn't insult your intelligence by coming up with some popular magazine type of "test" that claims to confirm your malady. No, life is too complicated for that, and the basis for your financial practices is too complex to use a simplistic method. Besides that, I would wager that you already know the answer. You've simply had problems acknowledging, treating and controlling the disorder.

As we all know, people tend to rationalize their behavior particularly if it is problematic. Now let's examine some other common explanations reactions to overspending behavior.

DENIAL

Frequently overspenders are in denial. "Who, me? I don't have a problem." Acknowledgment is the first step on the road to recovery. Hiding from the facts and ignoring reality will only keep you stuck in negativity and chaotic financial circumstances because it excuses you from taking action. If there's no problem, obviously there's no corrective action needed. How convenient.

SEX

That heading is always an eye-catcher. But here I'm not trying to be titillating or salacious, only informative.

You see a common myth is that women are overspenders and nothing could be further from the truth. It's not a male or female disease but one that's applicable to both sexes.

There are some differences of course, and the principal one relates to merchandise sales. According to the *Journal of Financial Planning* 23.8% of women report being "unable to resist" a SALE, whereas only 4.5% of men admit to that problem.

Insurance companies and investment firms are constantly surveying to discover differences in the spending and saving habits of men and women. General findings include: women are often more accomplished savers, more cautious savers, and more conservative investors than men. (Part of this is through the socialization process and part due to necessity. Women as a rule [despite the *Fair Pay Act*] continue to earn less than men with the same education and in similar employment positions. [An unfortunate historical fact.])

Women are also typically better at managing debt and credit, and declare bankruptcy with somewhat less frequency. Men tend to prepare better for unemployment contingencies.

Aside from the data concerning participating in SALE shopping there are far more similarities than differences in men's and women's spending patterns revealing we're all more alike than not!

"People who live in glass houses shouldn't throw stones" and in this society the vast majority (myself included) live in "glass houses" when it comes to spending. So instead of name-calling, stereotyping or blame affixing we should realize that men and women share this condition and probably in substantially equal measure.

Bottom-line, don't blame a proclivity for overspending on gender. It's just a myth and stereotype.

UPBRINGING

I'm sure you've heard of *Rich Dad, Poor Dad* by Robert Kiyosaki. In this best-selling book the author's premise is that wealthy parents teach good financial habits and practices to their offspring. Makes sense to me. If your father is a multi-millionaire you can learn first-hand, through observation and education, useful wealth accumulation strategies. Additionally, you will probably enjoy other advantages like an affluent environment and friends, better education, more opportunities, etc.

On the other hand if you learned money-wasting strategies from your parents instead of money-making ones you may be inclined to blame your upbringing.

Whether rich or poor, parenting is an individual matter. Rich parents can be poor teachers and poor parents can raise their kids to be successful, so blame yourself not your parents if you aren't doing as well as you expected. Further, according to the most recent data, as reported in *Money* magazine Millionaire edition (August, 2012 ed.) 81% of millionaires report their fortune was self-made while only 19% say they inherited their money.

EDUCATION

I'm a believer in education. As a college instructor I've seen how a business education can open students' minds to money management practices, stocks, bonds and other investment vehicles, advantages of passive investments, taxation laws, pitfalls of poor financial decisions, and prudent ways to more fully participate in our capitalistic system.

And, even for students who don't take a business major course of study, their education investment will typically benefit them with enhanced career prospects and income potential.

If you haven't a good education you are probably at a disadvantage. Of course when you see the number of successful people including millionaires and billionaires who are dropouts you may want to reconsider the lack-of-education excuse. And strangely enough, better education does not necessarily result in better spending habits. Instead, the better educated are over-represented in the overspender category. (See Appendix, page 85)

PLAIN DUMB LUCK

Yes, luck can play a significant role in the accumulation of wealth.

Moving to a favorable location or company, friendships with the right people, advantageous investments, etc. are all factors.

People "fall" into terrific situations often unknowingly. They might gain an inheritance, win the lottery, or make a spectacular stock pick. Or they could come up with a product or service that catches on and exceeds their wildest dreams or expectations.

They could have unforeseen career opportunities, friendships, or windfalls.

There are many success stories and all of them, if the tellers are honest, involve some unexpected good fortune. But blaming your financial difficulty on "bad luck" is just a coward's way of avoiding responsibility.

DISCIPLINE

You may use the excuse that you're undisciplined and lack self-control. Actually, that's a pretty good one.

We are in a financially undisciplined period in this country. The institutions we expect to be disciplined like banks, stock brokerages and the government seem to have completely lost their minds. The recent spate of bailouts, and ongoing revelations and scandals reveal a pattern of risk, poor judgment and lack of fiscal responsibility. You may think that because these corporations and individuals don't show discipline you're just behaving normally.

But the onus is on you to correct your mistakes. Through education, desire and commitment you can reprogram yourself for financial success and security.

NOT ENOUGH MONEY

People often say they don't have a spending problem – it's really an income problem. They complain that they need a better job or more money, but overall individuals and families generally spend approximately 90% of what they make. (see Appendix on page 85)   Some more, some less. However, the problem is the balance.

A mismatch between income and outgo is the difficulty. As we all know, our spending needs to be curtailed to the extent it can be met by our income, no matter how much or little we make.

After reading the preceding I'm sure you have a better appreciation for the difficulties of diagnosing and confronting your overspending.   The numerous symptoms listed in chapter one, along with the many psychologically based denial, avoidance, and rationalization mechanisms listed above make dealing with overspending challenging indeed.

And living in a society where overspending may be viewed as normal it makes things even more difficult. Maybe it's practical, responsible spending that's deviant. (Just kidding!)

As we will discuss later you may need expert, professional or supportive help to you make changes, and corrections that stick.

But whatever the eventual outcome, the courage to self-analyze, evaluate, and identify a need for change is further than most will ever get. It's too difficult to change and too easy to stay stuck in the muck of overspending, rationalization, and denial. So you will need strength and determination.

Chapter Three

MY CONFESSION

Ben Carlsen

MY CONFESSION

I'm still embarrassed by the decisions and actions which have adversely impacted my finances. I had a great start, an excellent education, a wonderful career, and made plenty of money. I had a family who taught me the "value of money" and the practice of responsible spending and saving. For years I used a budget, and maintained a regularly updated Net Worth Statement. I accumulated a reserve, had a 401K, a SEP (Self-Employed Investment Account), a brokerage account, real estate investments, etc. I owned my own home and vehicles.

Then I started making bad decisions. Risky investments, irresponsible purchases, excessive partying and drinking, irresponsible companions, and unhealthy relationships were all a part of the picture.

It was easy to do in L.A. where conspicuous consumption is the norm, and temptations abound, but I managed to maintain a healthy, if precarious balance-sheet. And I still managed to hold onto a seven-figure net worth.

However, things were about to change. I decided to relocate to Florida and purchased a home on the water, with a boat, a pool, a dock, Jacuzzi, etc. All the accoutrements. This was in 2000.

I had transferred all of my investments into a self-directed IRA at a major brokerage firm with a self-serving manager. When the dot.com, high-tech bubble burst in the Spring of that year I lost over 40% of my account balance. Also, I wasn't employed and I had opened a new business. Then more pain in the market, a move to Miami, and an emergency heart (triple) bypass. I had medical bills, was forced to close my business, recuperate, and reinvent myself. For a while I taught on-line for a measly salary, then I got a job at a local college making about a third of my prior income.

Then came the 2008 market crash that wiped out even more of my assets, afterwards the real estate crash that took away my home equity. My story is not too dissimilar from many of yours, I'm sure.

I can blame it on circumstances, the economy, etc. Or I can accept responsibility for what happened to me. I can begin rebuilding my career and my net worth, take some different directions, refinance my condo, and build new income streams. You see, playing victim will not help me. Taking responsibility and initiating actions will.

And, I suspect the same is true for you.

My parents and grandparents faced far more challenging situations then mine. They immigrated to this country with nothing, went through the Great Depression, worked hard in dangerous jobs for years. But they saved every penny!

I'm spoiled. Sure I can whine that I'm worse off than I was earlier in my life or career. But so what? There is always an opportunity for correction and a new beginning.

Vignettes

They say "confession is good for the soul" and that it's a necessary step on the road to recovery. So it may be good for my soul, and helpful to you to share my experiences.

I wrestled with the thought of how much self-disclosure to offer. However, I believe it's beneficial for you and me to open up and not keep our financial mistakes hidden. The following are a few of my true stories that you may be able to relate to, or at least chuckle at.

1) Unnecessary Purchases.

First, let me give you an example of overspending by making an unnecessary purchase.

I attended an auction of items owned by a company specializing in events, promotions and parties. I stayed for the whole auction and was proud of myself for exercising restraint.

However, close to the very end I spotted a lot on a table consisting of sea shells and coral. Now, I thought, if the price is right I'd like that coral. (I know how expensive coral is as a result of owning aquariums for numerous years.) So I bid, and I bid again.

I "won" the seashells and coral for $85 and was satisfied I made a good deal. I didn't really need all the sea shells but I thought I could give some to friends, keep some, and sell the remainder. The auctioneer said: "That was the buy of the evening!" He said: "It's worth thousands!" I thought it was more over-exaggeration and hype. However, when I returned to the auction house the next day to pick up my winnings, and after I boxed my coral and shells, the staff pointed under the tables to 15 more crates of shells! Astounded, I had to make 3 more trips to pick up all that stuff!

So here I am, up to my eyeballs in seashells in a compact condo, overwhelmed and trying to figure out how to dispose of all of it. Now you might say: "but Ben you didn't overspend, you got a great deal!"

However, the point is I succumbed to my excessive desires, spent money unnecessarily, bought things I didn't need, didn't even understand exactly what I was purchasing, and created a big problem for myself.

2) I used to pay the asking (listed) price.

I've purchased televisions, stereos, refrigerators, etc., at full price. Sure I looked for sales and tried to buy at a good price, but I didn't negotiate (except when I visited Mexico).

Finally, I learned to purchase other items just like when I was in Mexico or buying a car. The same principle applies. The seller wants to make the sale and get a profit and you want to achieve the best price, so let's make a deal!

I hate to think of the money I've wasted by not negotiating. Now I try to get a better price on everything. When I go to the movies I want every discount I'm entitled to. If I buy something at a department store I want to know if I can get a better price. Sometimes it works, sometimes not. Of course I don't haggle over buying a newspaper, or a hamburger, but I do try to get a discount on a haircut. Ask for every discount. They used to laugh at me when I'd go to *Costco* and ask if my prescription drugs are "on sale." Now they look for manufacturer's discounts for me.

Some typical discounts include: *Teachers, Military, Police and Fire, Senior Citizen, Automobile Club, Union, and Students*, but there are many more. It doesn't hurt to ask.

3) "Toys."

And here's another of Ben's follies. When I first moved to Florida I wanted a boat. Of course, doesn't everyone? So I searched for a boat, not methodically, but emotionally.

After looking at several and test driving (or should I say piloting) a few, I came across an ad for a 19 foot *Renken*, inboard-outboard, with sleeping bunks for two, sleek and fast.

The seller was a stockbroker (I should have known better) who said he was moving and had no place for the boat.

It appeared to be in great shape, was housed in a covered storage facility, and he assured me it was in excellent condition. Knowing just enough about boats and marine engines to be dangerous, we shook hands then went to the bank and DMV. He got his money and I got the watercraft. The following day I took possession and began the two hour boat trip to my home. Well, after about an hour the engine started missing. I figured it might need a "tune-up." It limped to my destination and there it stayed, for a while. I had a mechanic look at it, and the problem turned out to be a leaky water manifold. The engine had to be torn apart, the head and manifolds replaced, etc. Needless to say, I was pissed. I called the seller and his phone had been disconnected. Another unfortunate experience.

.

4) "Relationships"

Here we're talking about the romantic involvements that we all have. And I've had my share. Perhaps more than my fair share. And I know they can be very costly or remarkably synergistic to your financial (as well as emotional) condition. In my case I've been attracted to many who did not enhance my finances, and only a few who did.

I'm not complaining. I made these choices and money was not a consideration. Although for the most successful matchings I learned that it is. Oh well, I've had lots of good times. However, you would be well advised to interject a tad of financial realism into your choices for partners or spouses.

5) A Car is Transportation.

Yet another example…. While I was living in Los Angeles I was driving down the Santa Monica freeway and when I exited, I spotted a classic 1960 Bentley parked in a car lot. You know how they look: Big chassis, great grille, pearl grey and black finish, leather and burl wood interior. I was in love. "*Grey Poupon*, anyone?"

Well, it couldn't be financed because of its age, and I didn't have the cash, so the amicable dealer offered to lease it to me. This was my first and last lease! I eventually bought the lease out and owned the car free and clear. But I rarely drove it, and ended up selling it. Besides that I had three other cars and limited parking space.

And this wasn't the only mistake I made with cars. I love cars – less now than previously, but cars still fascinate me. Especially classic cars, sports cars and luxury automobiles.

You may find this hard to believe, but I've owned over thirty cars in my lifetime. This was, in retrospect, a huge, unneccesary, money wasting and counter-productive hobby.

6) Weekend Retreats.

Some people own retreats in exotic places. For several years mine was an apartment in Tijuana (Mexico). I spent scores of weekends there drinking and partying.

I rationalized that I deserved a break from my high-pressure jobs. Why Tijuana? It was exciting, seedy, dangerous and fun!

But my car was broken into several times, and I got into a few altercations. Needless to say, it had to end, and it did!

7) I like to eat out.

I don't cook and I have a "virgin" stove. For several years in Los Angeles I would go to a local restaurant in Pasadena for dinner and drinks. Often I would invite friends. I became a "regular" and knew everyone. The waitresses, the management, and the bartenders. I even ran a monthly "tab." At some point, I realized I was spending more than my mortgage payment each month at this local "watering hole" and "eatery." I had to reform, and I did!

I stopped eating at high-price establishments and began dating people who liked to cook.

Now I microwave breakfasts and eat other meals at moderately or low priced restaurants. (One of my favorites is *Chipotle*'s; great food, healthy and fresh at a low price.)

8) Homeownership.

I've owned many homes in several states. Although some were income property, most were personal residences. I would quickly tire of my house and look for a different one:

Bigger or better. Often I would put the minimum down, not get the best financing, and after a few years take out an equity loan. Dumb.

I now look at a house as a much more long-term investment, not a piggy bank, and a place of stability and sanctuary. Had I stayed in my first home in Los Angeles -- which I purchased for $22,500, with a $126 monthly payment - it would have been paid off years ago - and according to the county assessor worth half-a-million!

As an important aside, real estate has been a good investment for most of my life. However, as we all now know home ownership is a much more uncertain financial course these days. Take your time.

9) Addicted to bargains.

As we discovered with the seashell fiasco buying something because it's a "deal" is not necessarily a wise decision.

I grew up in a frugal working-class household where money was not wasted. Perhaps as a consequence of that mentality I gravitated towards bargain purchases. If it wasn't on sale, I wasn't interested. And, as I previously explained I am a firm advocate of negotiation.

However, this viewpoint can be dangerous too. Obviously you can't buy everything that's a bargain. If you try you'll go broke.

And, if you're a successful negotiator you'll create more attractive deals than you would otherwise encounter. So a quality that would generally be construed as positive can actually serve to your detriment. The solution, of course is to buy what you need and severely restrict your impulses to buy discretionary items.

I suspect I will never be a strictly logical consumer, and you may not either, but acknowledgment and acceptance of these weaknesses combined with a resolution to reform will serve you, and your budget well.

10) Messed up priorities.

Suze Orman offers an excellent guideline: "People first, then money, then things." Sometimes we get these priorities mixed up. We think we want something and buy it without thinking of the consequences to ourselves, friends, family or significant other(s). Or we buy stuff that jeopardizes our financial security. I readily admit I have been guilty of this. When times are good we think they will last forever. But that never happens.

My priorities were out of synch for several years, straining relationships and finances; forsaking long-term success for temporary enjoyment. It's easy to get confused in our society, because the emphasis is so great on money, status, and lifestyle.

11) I Didn't Respect Money

They say the best relationships are based on mutual respect. And I'm sure that's true. However, in my life I often considered money as an object to be used for my personal satisfaction. As you have seen throughout this chapter I evidenced utter disregard for money in some instances. It could be characterized as an "abusive relationship." Not one based on mutual respect, support and understanding. This may be the root of the problem.

Despite my disregard and taking the relationship for granted, my relationship with money has been my longest and most enduring.

Many of the people in my life have come and gone, died or left, fell out of love, become estranged, or moved away. But money (thank God) has always been there through sickness and health, through abundance and scarcity. Maybe not in the quantities I would have preferred but always around.

12) Unrealistic Plans for the future.

What's worse than a flawed plan? – No plan! I thought I was doing fine in planning for my gracious retirement. I had a substantial 401k, a modest pension, an IRA and Social Security. I had a plan. But it's easy to overestimate income and underestimate expenses. Life *will* throw you a curve. Many of them.

I'm always concerned about people who trust their future to fate, or the government. Who ever thought we would see all of the financial turmoil of recent years and an overall declining standard of living in this country?

Now I've shared just a few examples of some of my financial mistakes. I've also made plenty more. I refinanced mortgages when I didn't have to and squandered the proceeds. I lived large; larger than my means.

I overspent on restaurants, vacations, bought more expensive houses than I should have, and took excessive investment and retirement plan risks. Yes, it was an exciting ride. But my big mistakes are far behind me.

You may be thinking: "Why should I listen to this guy? And, you should be asking that question. Let me try to answer. I know the theory and practice of finance and money management. I have a business and education background, and have taught at the college and graduate levels in these fields. I've been quite successful and well-off.

More importantly, because I've been there (overspending)! I know what it's like. And, I have reformed! (Or at minimum, I'm recovering.) I'm not only talking conceptually, or from theory, I am sharing practical insights and advice from my own experience. Beware of those who proclaim perfection, particularly when it comes to finances.

You can learn from my mistakes and corrections. Particularly if you're willing to confront, confess and change your own.

Ben Carlsen

Chapter Four

MANIPULATION OF YOUR MIND

Ben Carlsen

MANIPULATION OF YOUR MIND

Have you thought about the underlying reasons for your overspending? Above and beyond the physical and psychological symptomology and etiology there is something else going on. The clever and pervasive manipulation of your mind and consumer behavior by major corporations and marketers is an incredible force.

I remember reading *Hidden Persuaders* back in the 1960's when subliminal and covert marketing practices were beginning to more fully emerge. Prior to the consumer marketing revolution advertising was pretty straightforward. A picture or drawing of the product, a description, and an explanation of the benefits along with, perhaps, a source vendor/supplier. The assumption was that consumers made rational decisions based on facts and need. But when psychologists, sociologists, and high powered marketing experts began to analyze consumer decision-making practices and tinker with the approaches to more effectively influence those decisions a new era emerged.

An era of marketing driven consumerism linked with image, social status, sexism, racial and ethnic characteristics. When the question: "Who are our customers?" was asked, targeted advertising followed.

Highly persuasive, but not easily recognized techniques are employed to create an internal motivation to buy something because it ostensibly would result in other benefits. The symbols and people used in advertising are not there by chance. They're placed there because of proven or speculated linkages and effects.

What does a handsome man or beautiful woman have to do with an automobile? The message is that you will be like them, or that people like them prefer this type of vehicle. So instead of that frumpy image you have you'll be perceived as "cool," "hip," "attractive," or "desirable," if you drive one of these -blank- cars. Of course we realize it's ridiculous, but the appeal is not to our conscious, critical thinking but to our subconscious.

This is not the only trick that advertisers use, of course. Famous people, Olympic athletes, movie stars, etc., are in regular view. Products are portrayed as exceptional, superior to other brands and necessary to our well-being. Brand allegiance is nurtured by logos and testimonials, endorsements, etc.

Awareness of these techniques is the first step in becoming more resistant to them.

None of us wants to be manipulated, particularly by strangers whose only objective is to get us to transfer our money from our pockets to theirs. And the constant barrage of advertising is effective in inducing us to overspend.

It would be a wise strategy to limit your exposure to advertising by trying to consciously ignore or disregard them. You can also critically evaluate and question every ad you see. Soon you will find yourself laughing at the clever but ultimately transparent efforts made by these purveyors of unwise consumption.

The marketing people are always one step ahead, however. And they are constantly developing new methods. The science of product placement, store arrangement, everything from store layout to aisle width to color and music is engineered to increase sales. When you visit the supermarket do you often find the arrangement confusing? Even blocked aisles do not usually happen by accident. The same with department stores and malls. Even the Internet.

Your shopping behaviors are constantly being monitored by sophisticated systems. How much time you spend at a particular locale, or in the case of the internet monitoring recording your site and url visits, associated searches, keystrokes, etc. are all recorded. And why do the stores want your phone numbers, zip codes, and offer discount or affinity cards? To increase customer loyalty sure, but more significantly to research your consumer patterns.

They want to know what you buy, when, and where. They want demographic information, whether you use cash or credit. If you're a returning customer and how often. Your product preferences and frequency of purchases. If you favor certain brands over others, etc.

You're nothing more than a rat in a maze to them. A lab rat to experiment on, train and manipulate. Perhaps it's OK, after all it's only business. And efficient cost-effective market data gathering may in some ways benefit consumers. However, I resent the intrusion and I want to be aware of when and where I'm being manipulated so that I can avoid or counteract it if I choose. You may, too.

Chapter Five

IT'S ALL RELATIVE

Ben Carlsen

IT's ALL RELATIVE

Whether you have a big home, a small home, or no home, it's all relative. If you go to work in a car or on the bus. If you vacation in Bali or the neighborhood park. If you dine at *LeBernardin* or *McDonald's*. If you go 1st class or have no class. It's all relative. Yep, we live in a relative world, and increasingly for good or bad, the basis for that relativity is economic and financial.

There's a litany of reasons why we overspend. Most of these reasons have to do with our Ego, self-image, need for love and acceptance, misplaced values, and desire to impress. There's a litany of reasons why we overspend. Most of these reasons have to do with our Ego, self-image, need for love and acceptance, misplaced values, and desire to impress. We "self-medicate" to temporarily erase feelings of inferiority, depression, worthlessness, rejection or inadequacy. Our drug of choice is often shopping. I'm sure you've seen the bumper-sticker on cars parked at the mall: *"When the going gets tough. The tough go shopping!"*

How did we get so screwed up? Gluttony is a sin. A deadly one. And we're gluttonous. Not everyone of course, but an increasing percentage.

Compared with previous generations we drive more expensive cars, have much more extensive wardrobes, live in much bigger homes, and have the latest technology.

A big reason for this may be our reference groups. Juliet Schor's study *"The Overspent American: Why We Want What We Don't Need"* (see references) identifies this as a primary source of overspending. Essentially, we tend to compare ourselves with others. And unfortunately we usually pick people at higher income levels. This makes sense when you consider it. Why would we choose to compare ourselves with the *less affluent*? However, when we do this we set ourselves up for problems. If we earn less we can't successfully compete in lifestyle except through debt and overconsumption. Feeling *"less than"* is not fun. But the solutions are even more onerous and self-destructive and they're not real solutions.

With modern communications and pervasive media we see much more of people's lives. Especially the superficial, money and possessions aspects. Obviously we live in a highly materialistic society. We've all been around people who seem proud of, and preoccupied with. Income, status and possessions. It seems to indicate a measure of their success and self-worth. And in a culture where materialism seems to be the highest goal and priority it's easy to buy into these false values. But what other values do we share? Is ours a particularly family oriented culture; with a shared religion or history, language, ethnicity? Nope. The principal shared value we have is financial. Status in this culture is conferred on those with more assets.

So it's easy to understand why we get sucked into consumerism and overspending. This happens at all levels of our society. Even the wealthy can fall prey to overspending – well beyond their often considerable means.

An excellent, although extreme example of excess gone wild is depicted in the film "The Queen of Versailles." This documentary is about a billionaire entrepreneur and his wife, Jackie, a former beauty queen and model. She has extravagant tastes and the couple are well underway in building the largest home in America. Bigger than the White House, and modeled, in a fashion, after the Palace of Versailles, with 30 bedrooms and 19 baths. At 100,000 square feet the couple had poured $100 million into the project.

The family lived very lavishly. Their trips would be taken in their private jet and they literally had warehouses full of art objects. The (seven!) kids had every toy imaginable, went to private schools, and had little concept of limits on spending. The family was the epitome of excess, vulgar, and conspicuous consumption.

Then came the "crash" of 2008, and a modicum of reality stuck home. They had to reduce their large household staff and eat at a nearby *McDonald's* (in their chauffeur-driven limo). But she would still go on shopping sprees although with perhaps less intensity. In any event, the movie is a great "case study" of excess. It's all a matter of degree!

I've been extravagant, and I'll bet you have too. It may be fun to laugh at the Siegels but we have our own issues. It's ultimately a matter of scale.

If you can buy a million dollar home or a jet plane or an expensive yacht why not? If you can afford it who's to say it's overspending?

Some people can't afford to buy a bicycle while for others a new *Bentley* would not be considered an extravagance. The objective is to live within your means. If your means are more substantial your spending can be too. Conversely those with more modest means should buy less. Where it gets out of whack is when individuals believe that they need or deserve to buy more or more expensive things than their budget can comfortably support. Or when they shop compulsively for emotional reasons. Or when they try to be phony and put on a false image of affluence.

If you sacrifice your savings, retirement, family security, education or future to buy stuff you're making a mistake. And, you may pay dearly for your irrationality.

Understand that you may not be able to afford what your neighbors or friends have (and they may not either!). Keep in mind that it's all relative. Relative to your income, relative to your needs and desires and relative to others. It may be some consolation that just living in America gives you a huge edge because our standard of living is so high.

If you broaden your reference group you can take some comfort that no matter how little you make, the poorest Americans rank highly by worldwide living and income standards. So don't fret, you're a winner by just living here.

Emotional purchases are more commonplace than we would readily admit. Two big-ticket examples are houses and cars. Yes you need a roof over your head but more often than not a home purchase is an emotional decision. Real Estate agents know this and will try to appeal to those emotions. Do you need the gourmet kitchen, the extra bedroom and bath? The pool; the Jacuzzi? Same with cars and car salesmen. Do you need leather upholstery, a sunroof, electric windows, etc.? Do you need an oversize SUV or a snazzy sports car? Do you even need a new vehicle?

As pointed out in Chapter 4 we've been seduced by the media to believe we deserve the best.

Actually what we deserve is the security and stability that responsible purchases entail. And, clearly the most expensive purchases may not be the best, or the best for us.

Of course we're not always buying homes or cars, these items are only the biggest expenditures. The obsession with more incidental items and the compulsion to own them is an ongoing dilemma.

Ben Carlsen

Chapter Six

TOOLS and TECHNIQUES

Ben Carlsen

TOOLS and TECHNIQUES

There are many strategies for dealing with the problem of overspending. The following tools and techniques may be helpful for dealing with your problem. Essentially this chapter is about treating your overspending disorder.

First get a MEDICAL CHECKUP. The purpose is to ascertain your physical condition and whether you have any of the medical symptoms we discussed earlier. A healthy body (and mind) is a big advantage in gaining control of your addictive behavior.

Create a BUDGET. Knowledge is power, and you need to know how much $$$ is coming in and how much is required for your expenses and obligations. Reduce your outgo by eliminating unnecessary or excessive expenses.

Just establishing a budget is not enough. Try to consistently adhere to your budget. If you can you will find it empowering, and a major step in financial responsibility. If you're married be sure to involve your spouse—and "no secrets." If you have children it needs to be a "family project."

Develop a NET WORTH STATEMENT. You need to know how much you're "worth," and what direction you're headed.

Keeping score is an excellent way to increase your interest and involvement in the Money Game. Your objective is to maintain a steady course of overall fiscal stability and improvement.

Initiate a SAVINGS PLAN. Spend less than you earn. Save and invest the balance. Try to save a minimum of 10% of your income. Invest the savings according to your personal circumstances (age, tolerance for risk, stability of income, etc.).

A super easy way to increase your savings is BofA's (practically) painless "Keep the Change" program which automatically transfers "change" – i.e. less than a dollar to your savings account whenever you make purchases that aren't even dollar amounts. It adds up fast.

Identify and ELIMINATE YOUR SELF SABOTAGING BEHAVIORS and label the underlying causes insofar as you understand them. Closely monitor your attitudes, decisions, and emotions as they pertain to your spending and saving patterns. You need to practice constant vigilance to prevent yourself from slipping back. For example, if your pattern has been to "buy love" you'll need to recognize that and substitute a more healthy way to relate. Your spouse, the kids, your friends don't necessarily view you as a walking ATM machine unless you've trained them that way.

Confront, reframe, and revise your destructive money attitudes and behaviors

Create a NEW FINANCIAL PARADIGM for yourself along with NEW MONEY MANAGEMENT BEHAVIORS. Consciously revise your attitudes and monitor your emotions in this area. See yourself as a responsible individual capable of attaining your goals. See yourself as a winner!

GET HELP if you need it. A psychologist, attorney, financial planner, CPA, money manager, relative, close friend or spiritual advisor may be able to provide advice and help. *Spenders Anonymous* or other self-help organizations might be appropriate. Or you may have multiple addictions. If you're a drunk you will have trouble controlling your spending. If you are a drug addict it will probably be worse. In those cases *AA* or *NA* may need to be your first step.

Sometimes you could just be unable, unwilling, or incapable of handling your finances responsibly. In this case, maybe you should turn decision-making authority over to a spouse, partner or even a third party like an accountant or money manager. (Hopefully one that's well vetted.)

WRITE DOWN YOUR EXPENSES and keep track of them. It's easy to let money slip away if you don't know where it's going. This may be a temporary exercise, or you might even continue it. I've done this and it's surprising to see how much money is spent and where it goes.

Most of us grossly underestimate our expenditures particularly those unrelated to recurring obligations.

There are applications for Smartphones that make this task much simpler than keeping a pencil and paper record.

REVIEW and BALANCE YOUR BANK STATEMENTS. Again, being an active participant will help you GAIN (or regain) control of your finances. It's very tempting to "let the bank do it" and many people do not even look at their statements. However, the more you are aware of and involved in the entire personal finance process the greater possibilities you will have for success.

PAY CASH. Study after study has shown that people using credit cards spend more. On average about 10-15%. It's just too easy to buy with plastic and to some people it seems unreal. They sever the connection between money and reality. Don't make it too easy to part with your money. With cash you will feel the pain when you have to shell out those "dead Presidents" on those little rectangular pieces of paper. See, you do remember it.

Use AFFIRMATIONS. Repeat phrases like: "I'm a responsible money manager." Or "I'm in charge of my personal finances." Or, "I control my spending." The repetition will make an impression on your subconscious and could help you change your behaviors. There is lots of anecdotal evidence and some scientific support for this approach to behavior modification.

Join a SUPPORT GROUP like *Debtors Anonymous*, or *Spenders Anonymous*.

The success of *Alcoholics Anonymous, Narcotics Anonymous, Overeaters Anonymous,* etc., offer validation to the twelve-step model and to the power of admitting to a problem, making a genuine effort to change, confessing to your weaknesses to others, etc.

EDUCATE YOURSELF. Read books about financial management like this one. Take on-line or college courses in personal finance. Read magazines such as *Money* or *Kiplinger's*, the money section of your local newspaper or *Barron's* or the *Wall Street Journal*. Begin focusing more energy on gaining knowledge and expertise in this area. Be sure to apply this new found knowledge and direct your energies toward responsible consumer, investment and money management behaviors.

EXERCISE DISCIPLINE. Small changes and successes can lead to bigger improvements.

Pat yourself on the back when you resist the temptation to make a purchase you'll later regret. "Buyer's Remorse" is a common affliction which can easily be avoided. Work on improving your "impulse control."

CONTROL SMALL EXPENSES they add up. Examine your daily expenses and see which ones can be eliminated or reduced.

You know the usual targets like household utilities, cell phone plans, using coupons, shopping for lower gasoline prices, buying generic products, etc. Also your work lunch, the *Starbucks* coffee, magazine subscriptions and newspapers (often they're available for free on-line). I'm not saying you shouldn't have minor indulgences and pleasures, just keep them under control.

THOROUGHLY EXAMINE THE NECESSITY FOR LARGE PURCHASES. Do you really need a more expensive house or car or appliance or television, or elegant jewelry, new furniture or overseas vacation?

MAKE IT A GAME. Saving money can be fun. Trying to get good deals, limiting your spending, saving money, and avoiding unnecessary or excessive expenses. Create a contest within your family to come up with the best ideas to save money.

ESTABLISH A RESERVE and closely guard it. You'll feel more secure in an insecure and unpredictable world! Financial experts commonly recommend at least six months living expenses. We've all experienced unforeseen emergencies and access to the necessary cash required to handle these exigencies is a valuable "safety net."

In times like we're experiencing a year's reserve may be safer. This is over and above your 401K, IRA, or other retirement savings.

ENJOY THE STRESS RELIEF that exiting financial chaos will provide. Financial security is an important component of emotional and physical well-being.

By implementing several or many of the strategies outlined in this chapter you will be taking charge, assuming responsibility, and feel more in control.

Ben Carlsen

Chapter Seven

CONCLUSION

Ben Carlsen

CONCLUSION

We've covered a range of possibilities in this book. Your overspending may be symptomatic of physical or mental disorder. It may be caused by a need to elevate self-esteem, self-medicate to alleviate or mask other problem areas in your life, or to feel better as a mood changer. We've also examined how misguided some of these notions are. We've discussed the external influences on your propensity to consume particularly as produced by advertisers. And, we reviewed the relative nature of spending.

We have explored a few examples of the behavior and discussed the relief that gaining control of your spending can bring. I've confessed to some of my foibles. And, we have looked at strategies and techniques to deal with the problem.

Now let me share with you perhaps the most powerful concept and strategy of all. Your overspending may simply be *habitual*. After all, you've been doing it for years, haven't you? Bad habits are hard to break. And learning new ones is daunting. Just like a favorite old shoe, we feel comfortable and secure with the known and familiar.

As I mentioned earlier, a few years back I had a triple heart bypass. This drastic surgery was a consequence of years of bad habits. Stress, eating too much, ingesting the wrong foods, and lack of exercise.

I still have some bad habits, but one I've successfully changed is exercise. I now exercise regularly-- almost every morning. And if I miss a day I feel guilty and bad. But instead of dwelling on my missed session, I quickly resolve to get back in the routine.

My routine is a result of commitment and practice. At first it was extremely difficult. But as time went on it became easier. And so it is with just about any habit. We can replace our bad ones with good ones and as a result improve our life, health, spirit, or even our finances.

My recommendation to you is simple. Make a habit of financial responsibility. When you encounter the impulse to buy something you think you really want, or need – pause, don't be so eager to part with your money. Consider the purchase and the sacrifice required to obtain whatever it is. Consider that your impulse to buy may be the result of mind manipulation, misguided priorities, or other emotional or psychological factors. Realize that it may be exhibition of a bad habit. Few purchase decisions are strictly rational in our society.

Begin a new habit of disciplined money management. A habit of restraint. People replace destructive habits with positive ones all the time. Whether it's diet, exercise, dental care, cussing, driving patterns, and many more.

If we see our behavior is non-productive, or worse, destructive, it makes sense to attempt change. No matter how daunting it seems you can do it.

In our culture, we're accustomed to having what we want when we want it. We have eroded our ability to say no! This applies to ourselves and our loved ones. It's high time to "get a grip." Begin by pausing and seriously considering each purchase, particularly the expensive ones. Resist the impulse to buy "stuff."

Everyone wants to sell you something. They want your money in exchange for their "stuff." But fewer want *your* "stuff." Just try having a garage sale and see how many customers will pay "top dollar" for your stuff.

We're a consumer-based economy. And you are constantly barraged with marketing and advertising, whether overt or subliminal. You have to be aware and strong to resist.

When advertisers will spend millions for a thirty-second *Super Bowl* commercial you know the stakes are high. Millions of us weak-minded individuals will succumb to their strategies.

You need strategies of your own and you don't have a high-ly-paid staff of experts to conduct the "counter-intelligence" effort.

You don't need to buy into societal norms of overspending and conspicuous consumption. You don't need to "keep up with the Jones's." As we've learned, you may be a rational human-being, but we all have our weaknesses and vulnera-bilities.

And, we're all irrational at times when it comes to some-thing as personal and emotional as money. It's a matter of degree. I'm certainly not suggesting that you live a Spartan joyless life of continual deprivation and denial. I do be-lieve, however, that responsible restraint is preferable to careless and excessive spending. Particularly when the consequences of such behavior lead to problems for your-self and your loved ones.

Look at your overspending as a bad habit. A self-destructive one. Then, resolve to change the habit. Start out by recognizing the bad behavior and beginning with small steps begin the process of modification.

Continue to replace your habitual overspending with a habit of responsible spending. And take satisfaction in your suc-cessful exercise of will-power and good judgment.

Or you may prefer to label your problem as an "addiction." There are plenty of folks who feel that way. And there are many similarities. I suppose it's a matter of severity.

There is some comfort in being an addict. Just don't fall into the trap of hopelessness or resignation. There are medical, counseling, and mental health professionals to assist, or organizations and self-help groups to join.

However, it does not excuse you from the responsibility and obligation to CHANGE.

In fact, for this specific purpose I recently initiated a resource website at: www.overspendersanonymous.com. This website will provide you with an opportunity to access helpful resources and gain knowledge and support.

I wish you well in your efforts to reform. I know the difficulty of trying to change established behaviors, attitudes and patterns.

I am confident that if you do the work: 1) seriously examine yourself and your spending habits, 2) read and apply the principles, strategies and actions described in this book, and 3) make every effort to seriously change your spending practices, you will make good progress. Best wishes for your financial success.

Ben Carlsen

Final Thoughts

It is my hope that readers of this book will endeavor to improve their finances and that they have found this material useful in that journey. We stand at a crossroads in America. For the better part of our two-hundred and thirty-six year history we have individually and collectively exercised responsibility and restraint in financial decisions. But for several recent decades our discipline has eroded and our confidence in the future shattered. For the first time in my memory a substantial majority of adults believe that their children will not enjoy a higher standard of living than they have.

The consumerism and excessive consumption paradigm may have run its course. The vast majority of us have far more things than can use or enjoy. It may be that millions of people will decide this lifestyle is not worth it; not fulfilling. The pressure and anxiety experienced by living larger than our capacity thinking "more is always better" is not a sustainable attitude or behavior.

Perhaps you have seen a little of yourself on these pages. Perhaps you will decide to curtail your spending and abandon the race to acquire the biggest, newest, best, and most. It's a race you can't win anyway.

If enough of us make an individual decision to consistently live within our means we might serve as an example for our neighbors, communities, and government. And I suspect our lives will improve as a result. I sense that Americans are getting fed up with overconsumption and overspending. We may be getting close to a "tipping point" in rejection of this dysfunctional model. You may be the one to make the difference. It all begins with a decision. Your decision.

APPENDICES

Ben Carlsen

OVERSPENDING BY THE NUMBERS

It's difficult to obtain what I would consider accurate, reliable and valid data about overspending. Obviously people are not typically candid about their finances and researchers tend to discount the accuracy of survey results. But a Journal article reported by the *AFCPE,* Association for Financial Counseling Planning Education and based on *BLS* (Bureau of Labor Statistics) data provides some revealing insights.

First, "the median level of the Spending to Income Ratio was 90%, with 39.5% of the households spending more than 100% of their take-home incomes.

"One fourth of the sample spent at least 121% of their take-home incomes, and 25% of the sample spent 66% or less of their take-home incomes."

-Overspenders had about half the mean income level of nonoverspenders ($16,946 versus $37,357).
-Overspenders had lower level of financial assets ($5,510 compared to $15,640).
-Overspenders were similar to non-overspenders in total amount spent ($25,021 versus $24,370).
-The two groups did not differ significantly in "other money receipts", which is not included by BLS in money income.
- The two groups did not differ significantly in amount spent for shelter or for most other expenditure categories.

-The only categories for which overspenders spent significantly more than non-overspenders were medical ($1,939 versus $1,460) and miscellaneous ($473 versus $304).

One particularly noteworthy and surprising finding resulted from a correlation of "overspending" with "education." The two were *positively* correlated. In other words, *a higher percentage of the more educated are included in the overspender category.*

CONSUMER RESPONSE TO THE ECONOMIC DOWNTURN

According to data reported by *Strategic Retail Mega Trends* "How America Shops" (in March of 2012) over 50% of Americans cannot afford the basics!

"Other survey findings include:

- 68 percent of those surveyed use coupons regularly, up 7 percentage points from 2010.
- 45 percent claim they only buy items that are on sale, also up 7 percentage points from 2010.
- 43 percent make a point to search online for store discounts before they shop, up 10 percentage points.
- 14 percent of women say they use their mobile phones while in the store to find a lower price before they buy.
- 66 percent of people pause before buying to ask, Is this a smart use of my money? Of those who make six figures, 47 percent say they pause before making a purchase.
- 58 percent say they stick to brands and stores they can afford. For those with a six-figure income, the figure is 36 percent.
- 48 percent stay out of stores where they might be tempted to overspend. For high income people that figure is 28 percent.
- 43 percent buy less when they go shopping, compared to 26 percent of higher income individuals."

(Founded in 1986, WSL/Strategic Retail is the leading authority on shopper behavior and retail trends.)

Ben Carlsen

CELEBRITY OVERSPENDING

I came across a celebrity budget included in a court filing in 2007 as reported by ABC news. This is an example of how "it's all relative," and how the average person cannot relate to "lifestyles of the rich and famous."

"Pop star Britney Spears spends an average of $16,000 a month on clothes. She spends about $4,758 on eating out, $10,250 on utility bills and $17,000 on automotive and other transportation costs. The clincher: She spends an average of $102,000 a month on "entertainment, gifts and vacation," according to court filings in her child custody battle with ex-husband Kevin Federline."

Ben Carlsen

OVERSPENDING ON "Exceptional Purchases"

"Breaking Your Budget? Why Consumers Overspend on Exceptional Purchases"

Consumers routinely overspend on unbudgeted purchases such as birthday gifts, car repairs, or luxury chocolates because they underestimate the overall number of such "exceptional" purchases, according to a new study in the Journal of Consumer Research.

"This tendency to underbudget for so-called 'exceptional' purchases occurs because, although each purchase is unusual in isolation, when combined they tend to occur with unexpected frequency," write authors Abigail B. Sussman (Princeton University) and Adam L. Alter (Stern School of Business, New York University). "People fail to recognize just how many items fall into this exceptional category, so they spend more than they would if they realized how often they were spending on these exceptional purchases."
The authors found that consumers forecasted ordinary expenses accurately but underestimated how much they would spend on exceptional products. Consumers were willing to pay more for exceptional items when presented one at a time than when they were presented all at once. "Consumers tend to treat each exceptional purchase as though it exists in isolation, rather than incorporating it into their budget as one in a series of unique purchases," write the authors.

For example, imagine that one of your favorite bands is performing nearby. The ticket costs more than you would ordinarily spend, but you have never seen this band live and decide the experience is well worth the cost.

Ben Carlsen

The following week, your TV breaks and you buy a really expensive replacement since you only buy a new TV once every few years. A week later, you are celebrating your 10th wedding anniversary. Since this is a once-in-a-lifetime event, you decide that the occasion warrants a splurge.

"Failure to aggregate unusual purchases leads consumers to splurge on purchases that they would view more conservatively if they understood these connections. Overall, this tendency results in overspending and under-saving," the authors conclude. "Understanding differences in accounting for ordinary and exceptional expenses can help consumers make wiser budgeting decisions."

Abigail B. Sussman and Adam L. Alter. "The Exception Is the Rule: Underestimating and Overspending on Exceptional Expenses." *Journal of Consumer Research*: December 2012.

OVERSPENDING and BANKRUPTCY

The following is an excerpt from a recent study of bankruptcies (in the state of Delaware) which found that overspending was the most common factor precipitating a bankruptcy filing.

Household Consumption and Personal Bankruptcy

From the Abstract of a study by
Professor Ning Zhu, University of California, Davis,
Journal of Legal Studies, vol.40, no.1, Jan., 2011

"…household expenditures on durable consumption goods, such as houses and automobiles, contribute significantly to personal bankruptcy. Medical conditions also lead to personal bankruptcy filings, but other adverse events, such as divorce and unemployment, have marginal effect. Our findings suggest that consumption patterns make households financially over-stretched and more susceptible to adverse events, which reconcile the strategic filing and adverse event explanations."

Ben Carlsen

RESOURCES / REFERENCES

Barron's, (online ed.) www.barrons.com

Carlsen, Ben, *Personal Financial Survival*, Miami, Palm Springs Publishing, 2011

CNBC, www.cnbc.com

Danko, William & Stanley, Thomas I., *The Millionaire Next Door*,

Journal of Consumer Research, www.jcr.org

Journal of Financial Planning, www.fpanet.org

Kiyosaki, Robert, *Rich Dad, Poor Dad*, New York, Bantam Doubleday, 1999

Maggio, Rosalie, *Money Talks*, Prentice Hall Press, New York, 1998

Money Magazine, (particularly August, 2012 edition - article "By the Numbers" pp.64-65)

MSN Money, www.msn.com

Orman, Suze, *The Laws of Money*, Free Press (Simon Shuster), New York, 2004

Packard, Vance, *Hidden Persuaders*, Ig Publishing, Brooklyn, N.Y., 2007 (orig. pub. 1957)

"Patients like me," www.patientslikeme.com

"The Queen of Versailles," documentary film, Evergreen Pictures, directed by Lauren Greenfeld, 2012

Schor, Juliet B., *"The Overspent American: Why We Want What We Don't Need"www.smmp.com/services/peace_justice_docs.*

Spenders Anonymous, *www.spenders.org*

The Wall Street Journal, www.wsj.com

USA.com (government info. on personal finance, money management, credit and debt, bankruptcy, retirement, etc.)

Yahoo Finance, *www.yahoofinance.com*

Zhu, Ning, "Household Consumption and Personal Bankruptcy," *Journal of Financial Planning*, vol. 40, no. 1, (January, 2011)

About the Author

Dr. BEN A. CARLSEN, MBA is author of several books and hundreds of articles. He is an educator, writer, businessman, manager, and consultant. "Dr. Ben," as he's known to his students, earned his Bachelor's Degree at the *University of Washington*, an MBA at *Pepperdine University*, and a Doctorate at the *University of San Francisco*. He has a personal and professional interest in management, economics and finance. Dr. Ben lives in Miami and enjoys exercise at the beach each morning, spending time with friends, and is a movie buff.

Ben Carlsen

If you liked this book here are some other titles by the same author:

Is it all a game? Are your personal finances part of a larger economic contest? Can you learn to play the game more effectively and win? *Money Game Winner* takes a unique new look at our attitudes towards money and taps into our competitive nature to achieve financial success.

Before you can improve your finances you must survive. *Personal Financial Survival* is intended for readers having financial difficulties and seeking to turn their finances around. Lots of tips and advice. Readers love this book!

Bites of Business is exactly that! A collection of "bite-size" articles designed to improve your business and managerial skills. It's all covered-- everything from customer relations, human resources, sales and profit, accounting, performance improvement and ethics. A great book for new, aspiring or seasoned managers

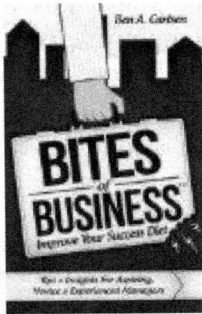

Available only in eBook format this short book lists the major (avoidable) financial mistakes that people make. These mistakes can ruin your finances – Learn what they are, and how not to make them!

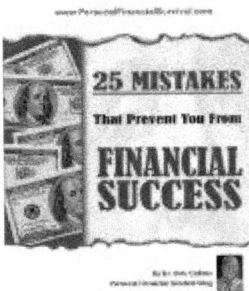

All of Dr. Ben Carlsen's books are available at Amazon.com.

Hardcover or paperback editions are also available at *BN.com* (Barnes & Noble) and, through Ingram Book Distributors, at bookstores everywhere.

"Money is a mirror. An examination of your money and the way you use money is a way of understanding yourself in the same way that a mirror provides a way of seeing yourself."

Michael Phillips
Developer of *MasterCard*

www.ingramcontent.com/pod-product-compliance
Lightning Source LLC
Chambersburg PA
CBHW031601040426
42452CB00006B/377